imago

JOHNS HOPKINS: POETRY AND FICTION
WYATT PRUNTY, GENERAL EDITOR

Other Books by Brian Swann

Poetry

The Whale's Scars
Roots
Living Time
Paradigms of Fire
The Middle of the Journey
Song of the Sky
Autumn Road
Snow House
In Late Light
St. Francis and the Flies
Companions, Analogies
Sunday Out of Nowhere: New and Selected Poems

Fiction

The Runner
Unreal Estate
Elizabeth
Another Story
The Plot of the Mice
Dogs on the Roof
Not the Real Marilyn Monroe
Huskanaw: A Novel
Ya Honk! Goes the Wild Gander

imago

poems by Brian Swann

Johns Hopkins University Press

Baltimore

This book has been brought to publication with the generous
assistance of the John T. Irwin Poetry and Fiction Endowment Fund
and the G. Harry Pouder Fund.

Johns Hopkins University Press
2715 North Charles Street
Baltimore, Maryland 21218
www.press.jhu.edu

Library of Congress Cataloging-in-Publication Data

Names: Swann, Brian, author.
Title: Imago / poems by Brian Swann.
Description: Baltimore : Johns Hopkins University Press, 2023. | Series:
    Johns Hopkins: poetry and fiction
Identifiers: LCCN 2022014726 | ISBN 9781421445670 (paperback ; acid-free
    paper) | ISBN 9781421445687 (ebook)
Subjects: LCGFT: Poetry.
Classification: LCC PS3569.W256 I48 2023 | DDC 811/.54—dc23/eng/20220401
LC record available at https://lccn.loc.gov/2022014726

A catalog record for this book is available from the British Library.

Special discounts are available for bulk purchases of this book.
For more information, please contact Special Sales at specialsales@jh.edu.

For Roberta, with love, as ever

Contents

II: Elegiac

III: Turtle Moon

Proem

⟶⟩⟩⟩ ❈ ⟨⟨⟨⟵

Locus

Transparencies of rain.

I open the top of the Dutch door,
stand in new air,
hold my breath
to know what breathing is,

waiting in place,
a bell hung
ready to strike,

eye wakened by
the dappling elm,
urgency of bird songs,
tuning forks,

a breeze lit from behind
delivers antique scents,
colors vacant and satiny
falling in on themselves,
trying to be what they are,

speech in the wind
raises small white flames,

crumbling Gothic carvings,
as if soul became all body
and was true.

In the wind all echoes
are equal.

Water is built for this, the sun
flipping in it like a tantrum while
five white horses dip their heads
calmly to drink.

Frisson of red skirts, a goddess,
poppies under the apple trees
where birds clatter
like boards. Look! The
moon is rising, Yupik
mask, carved dream.
I dream the light for night
to grow a single flower.

In the lake, sky come down for me
to swim in, stars fireflies
I scatter, sweep up

Northern Lights, ecstatic spirits,
bursting with scents of wintergreen
under the feet of bear and elk.

If you look long enough,
you're it,

as if at Cerveteri, augers turning
birds, beasts, stars to
human, prognosticating
the true cause and nature of things,
then on tombs painting it all
more vivid than life itself.

The moon wobbles over the horizon,
over the eyeless poult in the ditch,
garden turning back to an
echo of light.

In a corner of my window frame
three dead flies. In a pane,
a bee trying to return
to the hive, in another
old roses.

I open the top of
the Dutch door to small birds
flitting among red leaves like
demented minims, save one
who sits apart, philosopher
among the wits.

Swallows' shadows angle in
for a moment, then

even before a crack appears
in the sky they fly into it,
spinning out through nights
giving way to another horizon
into the nothing like a prayer
and beyond and we know they're there,
their solemn eyes a kind of light
reflected in the lakes.

Snow falls with no more substance
than a hunch.

Single things fall into
their own breath. Silence
soars in plain sight.

The vast breath of each cell
we call eternity.

Pines sway into absence grating
on flint sky, taut tart stars,
the perfection of the snow stretching
into sky as the river slides
ice up the bank, tossing light
in all directions, grinding
itself out, ringing dead ahead.

History

You can work it for all you're worth but it will still be
        whatever it is, calling across vastness in waves

seeming to stand still yet falling capaciously, moving
        into and out of its own shadow so it needs

no dimensions for light to enter at all angles, catch on
        anything, snag edges, flow over stone, filter

through trees with motes and minims as we try to find
        a way in since there's no way out, here where

you are part of the score, a kind of fiction, a presence
        making music of spelks and scraps that come together

like the music that made us, the dance of more than we are,
        or face to face, I make it, it makes me in a room

of mirrors facing each other spilling images like a spool
        of film on the cutting-room floor, frames unravelling

like streets that run into other streets, crisscrossing
        frayed threads on a broken loom, mirrors reflecting

flakes like quail in winter when you flush them
        and they merge with the snow.

Composed

Inside for days, gales whipping about,
TV with awnings torn from buildings,

cornices ripped from facades, pileups
on the throughway, downed powerlines

catching fire with worse to come. Who'd
go out in that? Not me. With the world

rearing up like Hebridean seas and no
lighthouse in sight, I'm best off where I am,

my wife reading Virginia Woolf, telling me
she's "amazed" by the word *composed*

to describe the small house seen from the
rough waves: "the composed look of something

receding in which one no longer has any part."
She says the word reminds her somehow

of years ago returning late, climbing the steep
driveway, turning the bend and seeing rise out

of the trees under Bearpen our small house
as if lit from within by last sun, the garage door

opening as we entered slowly as into the
composed calm of a completed thought.

Pulses

Stonecrop in the wall
   bright with rain,

yarrow, goldenrod stretching
   in all directions with

hardhack, huckleberry,
   steeplebush, thyme

I don't brush hog, cut
   or curb, each stem

a thought resolving
   along veins the rhythm

of antinomies as overhead
   light pulses vividly

invisible and stays
   for me to find, lose,

forget and find again
   and again

Them

In heat they open, four tiny spots, white,
 clustered, immaculate in a day loud
  as pronunciamentos. Bend down,

their tiny cymbals can be heard,
 a version of silence. I'd never noticed
  them before, under the stone wall,

beside the bear print in the dirt. "Ah," I say.
 But they don't last long, so I could allegorize,
  or say they're signatures, maybe Milton's

fugitive and cloistered virtue he could not praise,
 or music only insects hear, and now even me,
  if only a while, my own way.

Telegraph Wires

sail on, sagging comet tails.

Traveling light, they could be tall gods savoring

their own beauty. Nothing can intimidate them,
nothing offend. They touch and go, press close, stretch out,

strong and sturdy as trumpets, sober as flutes,
quiet as mirrors. Never completely themselves,

secret labyrinths, balanced and aligned
with other worlds, they leap intervals

like music. In an amnesty of shadows, nothing
weighs them down, and a million angels perch

on each strand stretching over the horizon to
where sky takes them in like cirrus,

drifting into halls that echo moonlit nights
before turning inward to ash. Here it may be cold,

it may be lonely, but on they march, vivid
in landscape, striding up and down, taking everything on,

cars and saints, babies, baubles and Dostoevsky
in a looping catalepsy, unending revelations.

Three Mallards

The gods enter as dust from a moth's wings, clatter
of pebbles in a mountain stream, from whisper of maidenhair fern

in fissures to rustle of Pleiades' plumage, as morning light's
silk thread on a loom, see, they return even under

bleared sky here on the bluff with its wind-turned, bent-
over hawthorn, as dunes moving when I move, a line of eiders

dipping over sandflats and out to sea on the cold coast where
I was born, Bamburgh Castle looming over rockpools' trapped fish

and crabs I watch on my knees as the tide reverses, sweeps in
behind more eiders three mallards on my grandmother's parlor wall,

line ahead, largest in front, smallest last, faked perspective,
forever

The Feather

I turn it round, and round, flash of sapphire, emerald, azure,
indigo, ruby, and more, each broken by the other so nothing sticks,
changed by glance or breath to endless articulation, and I look up

into the void whose breath's this spindly birdcall here in the back field
where I wish to slip the brokered self, eat the world simple and straight
from the garden that needs no pruning, no watering, where lowly worms

fill vast spaces with luminous exhalations, free swimmers in the pure deep,
no day, no night, going about their ancient office, turning death to joy,
clod and crumb to dream's largess and exultation.

Tropical Fish

Praise yellow, praise blue. Praise red
and all colors in between, excess
and outré too. But I never saw
such presence without consequence.

So what's it for? Is it vital to be
so visible, so bright, or is the aim
not to be seen but immersion in
what's there, like things that hide
in words?

Oh, tropical fish,
translucent as pure thought, immediate
as azurite or tourmaline, acute
and reverb as diamond's echolalia,
you flow by as light fractured and wavy,
alive in time lapse and after-image
translated into "fish" that make
new fish, lucid and resistant.

I.

The Garden

→»» ❋ «««←

Running

So I start, as if running was just going toward
or coming from. A dog howls like a siren

and I remember the war when I was born, beautiful
in its way, searchlights playing, barrage balloons

toys or fat fish, doodlebugs cutting out, falling
like stars over the shipyards, incendiary bombs fizzing

chandeliers in moonlight, our air-raid shelter
dug under the rockery, flowers overhead like a grave,

as if there were a life to come. And I run faster, here
and there, skirting and skipping, then slow down

as I head south until I hear the click of deathwatch beetles
chewing their way through Ely's ancient cathedral beams,

watch fine clouds of dust falling in stained-glass sunlight,
wonder when it will all collapse. I stop to feel the pulse

in wrist and neck, count it against my watch, because sometimes
you run into trance. I start again in an orchard,

another country. Something calls from the depths
of apple trees, in the blossoms, shaking and swirling them

down around me, so I sweep them up, hear the sound of bees
in branches under a flat sky where a large bird hunting

calls and keeps calling near a day-moon I could
catch and release, lost to time, in time, running

Nationalism

At first, I wanted to be English. I didn't have much choice.
The war just over, we sang: "The English, the English, the English
are best/I wouldn't give tuppence for all of the rest."
But everybody was English, so, since we lived near the border
and because my favorite Uncle Len had a Scottish name
that qualified me to wear the hunting Stuart tartan and a kilt,
I wanted to be Scottish. Then, on a family holiday in a caravan
on the Norfolk coast, I fell for two Welsh girls, both named Jones,
though unrelated. I was fourteen, they seventeen. I bought myself
Teach Yourself Welsh and decided to be Welsh until I made
the decision to return to my roots when I discovered that my
father's father's mother was one Alice O'Neill who left Cork
for England and was widowed at twenty-three with three young children.
The romance of this made me want to be Irish, so I read every
Irish myth and legend I could get my hands on, running home
each Wednesday at recess to listen to the BBC Northern
Ireland Light Orchestra play jigs and reels. So how did I decide
to be Jewish? With nothing better to do one summer, I booked
a seat on a flight organized by the university's Adventurers' Club.
When it was cancelled, all that was left was a flight to Israel,
which I thought was in the Bible until I got there, where I worked
on kibbutz Yad Mordechai, was fed yogurt and Zionism,
rode shotgun on a tractor, and fell for a sabra. I was Jewish
until, back in England, my Palestinian friend Yael was murdered
by Mossad in a case of "mistaken identity," which made me think
I should be Arab, or, later, Italian or Mexican, or just plain nothing.
Which was how on January 9, 1980, I swore allegiance to
the United States, becoming No. 108466898 and A13 834 018.

The Basil on the Sill

I wake askew in sun. A bird's one note
all night. A neighbor's C-flat scale, up and down,
going nowhere. Rise, stumble to the window
open to new towers rising over 9/11. Think:
If you frame anything it looks beautiful.
I drop my eyes to zinnias, roses flaring in a draft,
see shivering boys in clogs on cobbled lanes,
newspapers down shirts, faces red as the apple
I smuggled years later out of Chivers' prize orchard
for my father who hated apples but this one so amazed him
he wanted another. I told him there were none.
I look over the park whose railings are the walled garden
around that Victorian vicarage, one greengage tree,
a gooseberry bush, crooked crab apple, shaking teacups
in shaking saucers, the Rev. James's widow showing me
files for his *History of the Jews*. Thinking, *So that's how it's done.*
I want to be a writer. Instead, on February 13, 1955,
I'm "admitted to the order of Crusader knighthood"
until, "more interested in criticizing the Bible than
learning it," I'm cast out, and this is me now
inside sunlight slipping through panes, catching motes
in a cryptic dance of tiny moments, brushing against
the basil on the sill, each leaf 90 degrees from the next,
a quarter turn, spiralling to stars, dancing with Andromeda.

Bach in the Garden

"Air" and "Sarabande" I sing,
Glenn Gould minus piano, doors flung open, windows wide,
   chasing notes out among worms and swallowtail,
maple and tuberose, hoping "to be free of all the hemmed-in life"

   as I look up to the sun hovering like a hummingbird
in the curves of space-time with Bach, bigger than all of us
   yet ourselves, when I suddenly come to my senses and turn
back to the garden, its tanagers, milkweed and monarchs,

   rust-red thyrse of the sumac, and over all, everywhere still,
Bach the transformer who never left, so I get back to work,
   prune and plant here and now, tend the soil,
breathe the sexual tang of damp clay, while I hum Bach

   as I did when, scarce more than boy, I dug up our old field
just to show I could, humming "Jesu, Joy of Man's Desiring"
   to the rhythm of the spade, making time the way a musician
holds the whole and plays it out bit by bit, in my mind

   the garden already planted and harvested, fruits jumping
like bubbles to catch on the tongue or float like glass globes
   fishermen use to keep up their nets, until weather changes,
shadows grow like undertones spilling out of things,

   and I stop, look again into the heavens, where now stars flash like herring,
wondering if Bach actually existed, until I remember
   an old lady in the Orkneys who, when asked if she knew
who Shakespeare was, said, "Isn't that another name for God?"

Skunk

A white line, flight of small geese
    who live close to the ground and scratch gravel,
it's him, here he comes again, bobbling
    his walk as if it's hot, cooled by
his white ostrich tail, flowing at
    a constant speed, black nose alert
as ants, yes, he knows where he's headed—
    straight up the drive in his low-slung Packard
and into the garage for whatever fuel
    we've left, just the smell of garbage,
then back out without missing a beat, steering
    straight into the huckleberries then
the pines and is gone. But wait.
    When I look up, there he is, floating
like a cloud, a vapor trail in some subtle
    place of the mind, not missing a beat
at cloudbank or wind gust, fronting a storm,
    beyond whatever I make of him, beyond name.

Pastoral

I get up early, dress, walk into air free as the paleolithic,
   until I reach the village general store now just three sides
when one fell off, where someone squats and hides,
   grows only zucchini in fenced beds raised up high
on river cobbles. Two cars and a truck with flat tires
   sit in front packed with garbage. I continue on my way
past the DEAD END sign riddled with bullets, past
   the empty silo on the right, the farmhouse on the left,
roof fallen in, past the barn much bigger than the house,
   stalls empty, beams whole trees, home for swallows,
on I climb until I reach the abandoned ski slopes still marked
   "No Name" on maps. There's nothing here except
the swamp beneath Bearpen and the sound of distant thunder,
   so back I turn, like Wordsworth composing as I walk
sermons in stones, past dead dairy farms, glimpse shrews
   whose hearts beat faster than you can count, hummingbirds whose—
I round a bend and run into someone I'd never seen before.
   Soon we're discussing the weather, this and that, life itself
which I tell him I just read was a rearrangement of genes
   and molecules, "So," I said, "you could say we're all the same."
"I guess," he said, kicking a stone. "Maybe that's why
   they put the genes of fish inside tomatoes, pigs into anything
and God knows what into cows, and why not, since, as you say,
   we're all the same? And I suppose they still say we're

descended from monkeys? Still, I believe that if we can

do something I believe we should, like going to the moon,

if that *is* what we did." "Yes," I say. Silence. Then, "Have you

heard that guy in the cabin back in the woods there, over the wall?

He looks. "Blasts away all night at twenty-second intervals,"

I continue. "At what?" He shrugs. "I've heard," I say,

"he's a first responder who cracked up after 9/11 and came here.

I guess he's practicing to save us all from terrorists who'll

conveniently come at him in twenty-second shifts."

He takes a step forward. "You think it's funny? You think

I haven't seen you wandering about talking to yourself?

What did *you* ever do for anybody?" He spins around,

stalks back down the way he'd come, clambers over

the high stone wall into trees, and is gone.

Sonnet of Intimacy

after Vinicuis de Moraes

I could sing to her, *Whoopee ti yi yo*, g*it along little dogie*,
but she's no dogie, and I'm no Cowboy Jack. She's a Jersey,
more deer than cow, so the legend goes. I could give her a name,
Io, say, or Europa, for she has no name, just a number in her left ear,

333.3 is my lucky number. As I drive by I often pick her out.
There she is, I say to myself, and sometimes she'll pause
and look over. *What am I to her?* I wonder, and sometimes get out,
lean against the fence, hoping she'll come over. She doesn't,

preferring the company of her sisters. She's still a girl. But once
I squeezed through the gap beside the red barn thinking they used
to mix oxblood into the paint, and walked over slowly, so as not
to scare her, until I could almost touch her chewing her cud.

The smell of cow is delicious. Then, a hiss, a sudden stream,
another, two animals together enjoying a quiet companionable piss.

Shopping for Snacks

in Kingston Mall,
looking up into the girders of a building Walmart built
for a fleet of jumbo jets, I see sparrows flitting above

the produce aisles, skitting like sunbeams over the soft drinks.
No one seems to notice, not even when they begin to
argue sharp as lemons or sing sweet as apricots.

A whole jamboree's up there, twittering ghosts of the Esopus
before the Dutch sorted them out, except they're not
strictly speaking "sparrows," but weaver finches

not from these parts. Their messy nests under the canopy
of our doorway in the city look like the social weavers'
in the Serengeti's acacia trees. How can no one see them?

Perhaps they do, but it doesn't register above the *Sale* signs
and crowded check-out lines. Or they don't care.
There are plenty of the same birds hopping about

the hot parking lot, in abandoned carts or small trees
in concrete planters. I sometimes see red-tails in a city park,
unnoticed unless they're in nests with live video cams aimed

at their eggs or chicks. A pterodactyl might cause a stir, but
only briefly, like the coyote in Queens, the washed-up whale
off Harlem, or the three-legged bear up a tree in Bronxville.

I'd like to be a tastemaker or trendsetter so I could point
things out, but last time I did that, directing my neighbors' attention
to a hawk eating a squirrel on the Oval, they glared at me,

slapped their hands over their kids' eyes, gathered them
under their wings, and left.

The Moon Bridge at Ch'ien

There's a lot of rubbish here
    and an industry for it.
I pick out cans and bottles
    to redeem while crows
work the lumps and gulls
    turn things over, looking for
what they know. I too stick
    to what I know, which might
be a mistake since it's hard
    to keep tabs on the self
as it wanders about, now wind
    jamming up the sumac, shaking
sun-bits out of bits of glass, now
    squeezing groans out of a car
sitting in its bones beside
    a shirt flapping like something
you have to say while smoke
    drifts over fire reaching for paper,
Columbus's flight plan, a feather
    from one of Sir Thomas Browne's
ostriches, the core of an apple
    Jesus ate. There's a snake
somewhere. I saw its slough
    as I sat thinking of the kid

hanging out here when it was just
    an abandoned bluestone quarry
near a paved-over native path
    where stuff was dumped on
the sly before rules were drawn up
    and posted and it became an
official place where today under a sky
    tilting west I climb, or someone
like me climbs, to the fallen-in
    farmhouse on the rock lip,
the greenhouse with seasons all one,
    now collapsed and overgrown
with brambles, here where I'd follow
    vole tracks in snow into the moon's
warm green light, perfume of geranium,
    tomato, oxblood, where now I find
myself on broken glass above the distant
    dozer burying it all, quiet as that
Chinese girl I'd watched on the moon bridge
    years ago, looking down at herself in water
sheer as glass until she dropped a blossom,
    then a stone, then jumped.

A Bird

There's a bird, one note repeated in the rain
    as I lock the office door and head upstream along
tire-encumbered banks. They say Lewis and Clark
    came this way. They didn't. I pass the last Cherokee
"bent tree" hereabouts and strike inland for "Goldie's,"
    open 24/7. The same woman comes in
the same time each Tuesday. She works at the tribal
    factory that supplies plastic tomahawks
for the Braves. She sits beside me at the counter
    facing the bleared mirror's Booger masks.
"Someone said you'd drowned," she says. The others
    ignore us, part of a crew who think they have
enough work here for a lifetime. They haven't.
    The door opens and I hear the bird again, though
it could be a distant stump grinder.

The Garden

It just came at you. You were in it almost
without knowing— but let me dispense with confessions
and tell the truth: It wasn't that great, the Garden.
It just appeared from the street looming up after
you'd reached the edges and limits of more of the same.
You could even have been lost— "Tossed? Why tossed?"
Lost. Once inside it seemed smaller— "Or larger." There were
corners and benches handed over to nannies where
they talked on cell phones. No parents, just nannies who
passed around their charges, some ending up in branches,
others safe in prams— "Baby carriages." "Can't you shut up?"
Sometimes it snowed, sometimes it stormed, but nobody
seemed to think there was anything to worry about.
"What about the child molesters?" Trees made it feel safe,
and you were always in the shade and shadow of buildings
through which wind made sounds like crying. Sometimes
sunlight made it through and groped about. It looked
like hard work. "Work?" "Yes, what you do to make
ends meet." "Why on earth would you want ends to meet?
You'd go in circles." "Forget it." "Can I ask you something?"
No. "Why did you never marry?" Light slid around on the pond—
"You never mentioned a pond"—like water striders—
"Which are?"—shiny, fast, unpredictable beads and blobs
who dash about on the surface as if they're after something.

"Can't you see why a pond in a place with children
might not be a good idea?" I can now. "A still mind is
a calm, deep pond." The mind's a grave. "With ghosts." Why
do people have kids if they hand them over to strangers
almost as soon as they're born? Families are no more.
"What do those beetles actually *do*?" Who knows. I said
they were light on the pond. Metaphor. Flashing all over
like scattered thoughts of a broken mind. "Simile.
Have you ever been in love?" They look like they live
in constant anxiety, they can't keep still. "Can they fly?"
I don't think so. "Then they're trapped." They look like
shooting stars, or quick constellations. Some sink.
"Some shall not be saved. St. Paul." They're like pieces
on a Ouija board— "There's only one piece on a Ouija board— "
spirits summoned to give direction, help me cross the street
without looking both ways every which way, again and again,
unable to move—"Have you never loved anyone, even fought
to be affectionate?"—and go to my own house, my home
with its own entrance. "En*trance*?" OK, en*trance*, a place of wonder,
wife, children, a kind of fulfilment, where each thing means itself,
no confusion, who's who, echoes— "Geckos, you say?" OK, geckos,
by now one word's as good as another. Tire marks will do as well as truth.
"You had your chance. There's nothing more to say."
The Garden closes early and empties fast. It's lonely and scary
in the snaky dark. "Colubrine." Words, words.
Silence assails all in the end.

II.
Elegiac

The Screen Door

Legs ridden all over, point to point, fair to furbelow,
now useless as a whale's.

I who once moved like breath am now
connoisseur of pratfalls,

bounce house. But
yes, I say legs and knees may be arthritic

as barrel staves, but the mind still counts,
and with it on board something

might be done to move through the world again,
this time taking nothing for granted, gratefully,

religiously almost, like those venerable maples,
hollow, but still urging out green, those old stone walls

coursing across fields, pulling hills together, heading off,
while night wind is music on the broken strings

of my screen door.

Making Sense

Age had made the idea of death as familiar as
the idea of life, so I decided to make myself

comfortable on death row while I sat on a bench
waiting for the doctor's office to open but when

it did there was no doctor just a nurse practitioner
who had the day off and it wasn't a doctor's office

anyway but a veterinarian's and he was out on a call,
which was OK because at my age I was ready for

anything and have a theory for just about everything
such as you cannot think of the dead because you

always end up thinking of them living so the only
thing that makes sense in this comédie humaine

is that there may be death but there are no dead when
the vet returns and tells me there's nothing wrong that

a change of litter and diet won't cure so I go home,
pour a stiff one, and it all starts to make sense.

Jokes

Was Blake serious when he said he could not
consider death "anything but a removal from
one room to another"? If so, or even not, I'm
wondering which one I'm in as I gaze out at nothing,
a plaque of white, one slow shadow merging into
a snowdrift after a night when a bug crawled
into my ear and I thought I was having a heart attack,
the way my father died after trying to live forever
with congealed beef fat thick on bread which
he made me eat too and which, I'm sure, gave me
this angina, a girl's name, another joke, like
what happened to my teetotalling Uncle Ted who,
they claimed, fell drunk from his oil rig and
was never found, or his wife who hanged herself in
a heat wave, dangling like a puppet I was too small
to cut down and I laughed, like the time I fell into
a Talkeetna snowbank, sank way over my head,
kept sinking the more I struggled, nothing to push
against, and when they pulled me out I was still
laughing at the Giant feeling around the dark room
for Jack, the way we used to catch catfish by
the tail under the bank, fee fi fo fum.

The Code

I had just been to see my father where
  the wind sat like a clapped-out motor
and a lake smelling of burnt wood shavings
  plugged the background.

In the silence my bloodstream droned
  behind the high hum of nerves until day
moved to the edge and tipped over
  on him who when he saw me
switched on the TV, changing channels
  until he found cartoons, one with a car
driving off a cliff, another with myself
  saying the opposite of what I wanted to say,
meaning the opposite of what I said, so
  deciding to say nothing in a code where
each prayer was a curse, each thought
  a scream, and nothing was symbolic,
just itself.

The Silence

I watched my father disappear
  into the furnace and come out

ash I gathered in a jar and kept beside
  the mantel's brass monkeys looking

through the window to the yellowhammer
  chipping fast as my father's *tap-tap*

so our shoes would last forever,
  steel-shod with heel and toe plates,

built up with spit and polish so they
  shone bright as songs of the Himalayan

jay thrush he'd heard, each bird
  in pairs singing faster and faster

until they overlapped as the jungle
  darkened and disappeared, like him

who drove through his headlights
  into the silence beyond.

Elegiac

Windows Askew

Peepers, greens, bullfrogs fading as a thrush sings on a rung
beside the windchimes. A robin sits on the empty feeder

looking around. The maples' red twigs hang above the over-
grown garden, and again I watch her drift along stone walls

under the huge, battered line-trees whose cracked limbs still
sprout red florets delicate as orchids. But she is not looking at them,

and not back at me, as she turns off near the abandoned
farmhouse held up by planks and briers, its lone carp rising

gold through water that was ice, coming up slow, like a question
to which there is no answer, and she's gone.

In the dry streambed a porcupine, scratching, working himself over,
moaning. Soon I'm scratching too, both of us moving with

the dull monotony of grief. He makes no concession to silence,
shaking his quills, sniffing bark until, half-hearted, balanced on his

earthbound tail, he starts heaving himself up a tree, but falls
back in a heap, spinning round to see who did this to him, then

comes straight at me, sniffing the air, tiny eyes not much help,
groaning as if everything hurts, and I groan too as he trundles

past like I'm not there before shooting up unstable scree,
still scratching, grief transformed to speed, and he's gone.

Anonymous still, I make do with feints and figments, fragments
in a light eerie as phosphorescence from the split fish or pilot-whale

strips we'd watched them hang, looked through to the Dipper's
seven stars and its bear tracks heading past the pole star sitting

like a quail's egg. Sadness everywhere like air under a butterfly,
barely keeping it afloat.

Fresh drifts, shifting integrities, snow losing itself
in the shape it inherits, here where our house endures,

wood warped, windows askew in a trance of sunlight
acute as absence. A sort of duress keeps everything

in place, a structure from which has passed the desire
to be something else so there's nothing for shadows

to feed on, make more or less, here where light lives
trapped in mirrors and her glass figurines so they're

still on fire, here where nebulae spill over old boards
and furniture that memory grows from like old flowers, and

the pole star turns above logs in the hearth, maple and cedar,
cherry smooth as eel skin, everything its own emptiness, here.

A Bird

The streambed's strewn with garbage and broken bottles.
A torn shirt hangs from an uprooted tree and—a flash,

you can't tell what as morning grinds out light,
and I remember a hummingbird in the grass here,

holding it up to my breath that ruffled its feathers
so they shone the way thought can glimmer and

be gone. I push open the garden gate one last time,
pick a small jade tomato, let drop. A chickadee hangs

upside down in the bare shadblow that snowed
each spring. I listen: a bird's song, silver wave on wave,

dying away like breath from a mask. I try repeating it
in case it wasn't there.

Spectrum

Dawn veers over the mountain, down
steep pastures broken by stone walls, through

stunted juniper and low thornbush into the house
where cluster flies wake in sunlight and scream

at high windows to be let out. Days still demand,
so I get up, make the bed, drag the comforter

over where she used to lie, though now each
morning when I reach over nothing's there. But

I feel she will return, lie down, get up, rhyme
with table, chairs, floor, the spectrum split

on the ceiling, over walls, from the crystal candlesticks
she won and which, in the dark, still work.

The Photo

The watch goes off in my desk. I open my eyes
to the photo of her standing on the stoop,

each morning looking back at me. Out the window,
nothing moves until a bird flits by, no sound until

a dove mumbles and a gun fires, just as the compressor
in the fridge goes crash. I see a spider moving across

the ceiling, a wolf spider, the kind that jump from ambush.
Another is hiding behind the photo. All night coyotes,

wild and hungry, roaming through town. The photo moves.
I see her on the stoop that still needs fixing. The steps
are loose. They'll stay that way.

The Necklace

Delicate sterling links tiny as tremulos, now a tangled mess.
Untangling, everything came out worse, "station beads,"

baubles like tiny acorns or glass balls to keep fishnets up,
as confused as the rest, a star, snowflake, dove with olive branch,

rough glass emerald signifying something, and the Evil Eye,
all part of an endless knot, but there had to be a beginning

and an end, a way in and a way out, not necessarily
in that order, but pull, push; tug, shake; and whatever

was loose tightened up again as if it were never meant
to hang or sway. But she kept at it, I kept at it, into nights

and out mornings and then, when I came home one day,
there it was unraveled, laid out flat in a circle on the desk,

neat as if a brownie's work, and a note: "I stopped trying.
It just seemed to do itself."

Eternity

I'm watching light sift on fading wild roses,
wind filling my shirt forgotten on the line

as if somebody's in it, then turn around to
my wife in the mirror's crystal void who

says she dreamed of eternal life again,
then I get up and spend the day among huge maples

rotted out yet growing, loose stone walls pulling
hills together, puffballs released at a footfall,

fields full of dung full of worms for the garden's
hardpan I'll work till loose, eyes everywhere in

the full-on force of the land till skies swoop like
Van Gogh's over fireflies blinking in blue-eye grass,

rustlings in dry leaves, and I return to the deck
in need of paint, a cecropia moth pressing

its crescent moons against the screen door, the
living room now bright as the moon, with my wife.

Grief and Magritte

I put the photo back on the wall beside the Magritte drawing
of a brick wall, watch slow rain drip from the lintel,

shadows, and a ghost moon over the maple rooted in the stone wall,
all of us snagged in a net whose skeins tangle in night sky

where one star dreams another until morning grinds out fire
burning into the world like grief, where I walk alone among rocks'

harsh rhythms set down in my garden as datura and dogwood
swans fly over, heading north in a formation cold as their constellation

while a gust hits the first swallowtail, knocking it out of air,
and the stream in spate leaps from wild, quarried heights,

hurling off spray going everywhere and nowhere, while summer
spreads from a high, stained-glass window with notes like

the nightingale in our Kanlica garden barely big enough for us three
let alone a bush and the moon that drew the Bosphorus up to

our old yali's high wall, making time's voice bleaker than the words
that now drop onto my notebook on the old oak desk, the moon

behind it all going down headfirst, a spinnaker billowing in the open shell
of pure space, a memory grating along the inside of my skull, a woman,

and a child's echo—*What is the moon? Where did she go?*—and I stare
at the wall with its drawing of a wall and caption—"un objet

fait supposer qu'il y en a d'autres derrière lui"—and there is nothing.

The Dog

I'm looking into the mirror that faces the window
in which everything flows back and forth, in and out,

one and another. I feel looked at by my own reflection
so I go out and look at a tree. Before I looked at it

it could have been anything. Now it's tree-and-me.
Back inside, I turn on the radio. Turn it off.

I'd emptied the garden. Now I inspect the last
green tomatoes on a table covered with squash.

A crow calls through the glass. Another replies.
I rouse the dog, turn the radio back on. Gluck,

"Dance of the Blessed Spirits"? I open the door.
Late autumn sun floods in. How far can it go?

Everywhere, until the moon is up, flinging bits
of herself out into the void whose breath's an owl's cry,

whose light is fragrance white as hyssop. Earth opens
to her, and I follow, the dog at my side. What's he see

as moonlight flows across my body making another
me to the side? He runs off as night birds call. I call

back. The dog returns, drops something
dead at my feet.

Death

One minute sailing through the blue,
the next it reared in the glass and

hit her, so now she lies on her back on
the deck under the window, soft white breast

round and still, legs twitch, grasp at
nothing, stiff as those mechanical birds

when I was a kid that sang on their perch
for a penny. I don't want her to join

the flicker I'd laid under a stone in
the wall, goldfinch or hummer whose

colors I still feel on my palm, shape
so perfect, so detailed it looked constructed,

and, though death is private, I stand
staring at the phoebe as if she had an answer,

and remember a young porter gazing
at the naked white body of an old lady

on her back, alone, trapped on the morgue's
marble slab, silver hair unbound, long

legs splayed, and I could not take
my eyes away, seeing it still, the

attendant hosing down the concrete floor,
bits of flesh stuck to yellow rubber waders,

then sitting down to eat his sandwich lunch
right there, on a chair in the cleared space,

the blaring light, grotesque sun
in that flat white sky.

The Same in All Directions

On my windowsill, my grandmother's Victorian
paperweight. Inside, one bubble poised forever at the tip

of a pansy petal. Other bubbles are galaxies peppered
here and there round her favorite flower, pansy, "thought,"

whose saffron streaks look hand-painted, floating
like a tethered astronaut in the artifice of eternity

which I look over and past to midwinter snow
sitting like bleakmindedness until, in a flash, light

rings, grass spurts, trout flash, and the field's a razzle
of butterflies, sky a field of sunflowers, until stars

give off scents and the moon turns over, flips in
the lake's shivering mirror, the same in all directions,

which I will enter quietly, steering stars aside, hang
weightless as a bubble, floating in eternity.

William Blake and Space Travel

I seem to have used it all up, there's
nothing left. Revisits do not unlock
any doors that might have been hidden,
windows I might have papered over or which
had melted into the wall. This is cruel, time.
Why is there so much cruelty? Is everything
throwaway? Who has been left to molder
under old floorboards, in old journals?
Flashes die out or plug away like
tired fireflies. What I have left is ludic,
lunatic, like being at the edge of the desert
in the desert museum you have to pay
to get in to see desert otters in concrete ponds
or lizards posed like billboards, packrats jerky
as robots. "Can we write about robots?" was what
a student had asked. My silence upset her.
I nod my head, a bobble doll. "Sure. A Czech word."
Who cares? I'm not a sympathetic type.
Someone once called me "a shrinking violent."
He lived in a windowless studio in the East Village,
kept unwashed dishes in the bathtub, loved cricket
and baseball and was deaf in one ear. As I think
all this I'm watching my two dogs at the end
of the driveway digging dirt and eating it.
On TV I've seen elephants do this, for minerals,
the voice says. Babies do it. I did it.
I still remember the sharpness of one handful

and the sweetness of another. I also ate dried snot
and earwax, enjoyed squishing gumboils so
the contents spread over my tongue. The world
was delicious. I still like the taste of blood,
my own smells. There's a plant, I read, that blooms
once a century and has a terrible stink that insects or bats
can't resist. Some others smell like shit and are
also irresistible to bat and bird, their stench a splendor
in air. Now each night I call out names that drift
like scent but they're garbled, words clashing or
grating on their hinges. I keep at it the way
a dog digs though what it was after had escaped
long before. Besides, the dog is not hungry nor
the rabbit afraid. One doesn't know he's a dog,
the other he's a rabbit. But there's so much to know,
so little time left, and meanwhile rockets are readied
to escape to the moon or Mars, portion out rocks,
make water for plantations tangible as Ireland or Virginia
by discoverers who know the sun is money,
a golden guinea shining while the same old heavenly host
still cries "Holy, holy, holy."

Theater

Someone left the lights on. In the dark they flare
like flowers caught by glass panels and thrown
onto the stage. I can see faces as I walk among them
sweeping, picking up, poking at flames that don't go out,
rehearsing in my mind a plot that doesn't quite come together,
words that don't quite come through amid a tangle
of ropes, flats, and pulleys, scenery left hanging when
the painters quit and forgot to douse the lights

Light

Dawn creaks so slow I could
wring light out faster myself.

Stones stretch to fix their shadows,
hold their breath until it's time to

curl round as the land darkens again,
heaves into mountains where birds

push distance into purple smoldering
like gentian where I watch dark figures

moving off, and follow under startling
star routes until, far off, I see a house

much like the one I live in but compounded
of light too bright to see, and go in.

III.
Turtle Moon

→»» ❋ «««

Bats

are mice who went wrong
way back but flapped about, cutting

and pasting, adding and taking
away, until they got it right, so now

any mistake's no big deal as they
do things their own way, sleeping

all day in attic and eave, coming
alive at dusk, intense morphemes in a

vast sentence to feel and feed
off the dark, make sense of night,

returning at dawn to tie up to
the same spot, dig in claws, wrapped

in wings, settle down beside us,
and we might not know they're there.

Serenade

But still we can get to know the heavens, for instance,
  by hoisting the moon back the way we found it,
giving the tired sun a boost up, replacing the planets
  in their slots, easing out a few just for kicks,
and to balance bright asterids up there placing a shadblow
  in bloom down here, even stirring clouds in a swirl
round Jupiter, flicking sunflower spin-wheels
  at the center of black holes, and there it is,
the universe laughing at itself and me laughing
  at myself standing by the window watching birds
haul themselves out to rest where night claims
  any light left in the deepest parts of trees until
it too is swept with its stars and moon like a flower
  into moths' antennae, throats of spring peepers,
a new world reflected in the eyes of mice.

The Passion

Spray hangs in the air as waves the size of men
roll in on top of one another near the fishermen's shacks
and drying sheds. Birds fall from the sky, settle on roofs,

on salt-eaten trees, sounding like the crackling of fire.
Men come running with sticks, stones, shotguns.
They yell, throw, shoot until the flock rises, fraying

at the edges, bits falling off as it wheels inland over
the lemon trees, over the church, blocking the sun
until in the distance they could be anything. A dog

beside me sniffs bloody feathers a man kicks aside.
Everyone returns to town where thorns are pressed
into Christ's head. Blood blinds his eyes. Pushed out

and beaten, whipped, he staggers, falls, rises to more thuds.
Blood soaks his purple robe. Flies land. A chicken pecks
the dry splatters on his feet as he is shoved and pulled

into the church. Sobs, then everything goes quiet, until
he reappears as the life-size wooden figure hammered
to a wooden cross men carry past empty vendor stalls.
A rooster crows, and what's left of the flock returns.

Churchyard

Words in stone I can
still hear, just, or see

their shadows holding in
breath so as not to be blown

away here where sermons
in stone are rare now but

sometimes their spirits
fly about doing their best to

turn the world around, shake
and right it to come again

fresh for you, young
at the hem of time's

long shadow, the sky
forever full of signs and

surprises like frost at night,
or the sun in the morning.

Why

        when this unbeliever sings in the choir
doesn't lead melt the roof, stained glass
drain, and at "spem in alium" organ pipes
fly apart, fan tracery fall like feathers,
smothering the sonorous scent of beeswax candles,
and the score in my hands crumble into echoes
of recalcitrant dark, and what will be left
of wonder when the singing has to stop, and
what remain when disbelief has gone?

As With a Child's Eye

Morning's glass. Finally, after weeks of fug,
the wind shifts. That's all it takes. Silence

slants in too, clean, along the rocky shore,
as small waves erase themselves while

shore birds call and answer until no calls,
no waves. You get used to things being like this,

first something, then nothing, their way
of shaping things, a rhythm, the same way

l sit and gaze through the window back
into a child's rock pool where water was sky, blue, blue,

nothing in it, which was why it was blue and
went on forever, so full it could have come

from anywhere and nowhere, where everything was
the same, so nothing could scare me.

North

Peneplain of granite, gneiss, schist.
Lands cut over, abandoned.

Small dunes run on standing still.
Alluvial fans are an insistent voice

where in first light flesh blooms
and glacial roses nose up through flagmarl,

ice-gouged. Moraine, esker, drift, words-
things. I breathe loess, draw in the

breath of trees while the lake turns warm top
to bottom, cold bottom to top where

loons the luster of chert dip, and pause.
A windblown rock-flower roots deeper in

this soil than jack pine whose laterals slip off
bare rock where lichens hunker and moss leavens,

where sky reaches down to blood locked in ore
and the fire in the grate of old birch heartwood.

Silence

Which way the day goes depends
on the winds and where
it ends depends
on their shadows and
where I've been depends
on words which are always
too thin
and
too quick so
I'm left grasping to snag
their skins
and crawl inside
and
go back into dream where I wander
about wondering who's
the original
and
who's the Aztec impersonator
and who's wearing who

Until
I wake in the dark, wordless,
throw on some clothes, go
to the door sure
I heard something like the snap

of bone, click

of manacle, fading barks of dogs,

and push the door open

slowly,

thinking I see dark figures moving,

rousing turkeys in the draw,

and I set off

under dimming stars until in the distance I think I see

a house much like the one

I left but too bright to be visible, so

I return and begin my day, another day of

picking at myself

chewing nails down to nubs, filing

and shaping,

squeezing pores,

scratching the scalp bloody,

clipping, shaving, gouging,

trying it seems

to dig myself out to a wordless core, as if

something's there, or vanish the way

my father did, sticking blades into his ears,

working himself into bottles like a four-master,

or my sister cutting herself, or my mother

addicted to enemas and neti pots

while time goes by as spun glass, shining echoes,
rivers on which 1 drift downstream, floating over
drowned towns whose voices rise and
flow around rocks, form figures in smoke,
shadows of the shadowless,
and when 1 look up there are
trees expressing sky with migrating birds,
until the polestar
turns, grinding from eternity
time in which
a year's a month, a month a day, a day an hour,
an hour a minute which is enough for me to listen
for the hermit thrush who each day
prays the sun up out of the ground, floats it over
the rough wall
that opens flowers of the trumpet vine, here
where time drifts beyond itself, and keeps going, silent.

Butterfly

Sleepless, I get up,
check the mirror
for me, look out

the window through
light eerie as
phosphorescence

from split fish, drift
over the tundra
to the Dipper's

seven stars, bear
tracks heading past
the polestar

which sits like a quail
egg, nothing holding
it up, the way air

under a butterfly
keeps it afloat

Imago

<blockquote>
on its way through the changes, the patterns
</blockquote>

of what led up to it, the catches and releases,

as if it didn't know where it was going,
and didn't have to because it was going there

anyway in its own time from when I first
came across a leaf with eggs, put them

in a jar, watched hatch, crawl about, expand
and look around as if rhyming with themselves

saying now, and now and now until they're
gold lamps hanging, splitting down the back

to release what was always there, which now
gathers and flies off, lightened images in air.

The Wind's

leftovers   bygones   tuning fork   fits
everything everywhere   no diversions   fills the incomplete
expands the excessive   incomplete as desire
raises the useless   stakes everything on itself
no hedging   resolves the unseen   shakes shadows
drives the discarded   uproots whys whats and wherefores
resolves the various   evidenced in effects   known by results
the unseen hand

A Sleeping Rock

after Jonathan Edwards

Night shakes stars.
    A shower like small bells.
Distant lightning, flies on Chinese silk,
    glass flowers in a ghost's hand,
 until morning shakes
    waves and gulls wheel
over surf leaving pebbles
    and shells high on a beach
where a single rock
    wakes to the nothing
it thought it had forgotten.

Turtle Moon

Pig moon, full moon of the feral sow on a bed
    of last year's leaves who nuzzles her newborn
struggling in the brief letdown for the richest teats,
    milk rich as the sea.
                    This too is the turtle
blood-moon, moon of the loggerhead that paused
    in silt-weighted waves to smell the air before
hauling her carapace past waiting ghost crabs
    into low dunes where she chooses a spot, scoops
out a pocket, settles herself, goes into an egg-laying trance.
    Soon one, then many white globes drop from her
till, tired, she pulls back the sand, tamps it down,
    scatters her traces.
                    Deep in the dark, germs
of life are floating slowly to the top of their yolks,
    hanging over their rich ocean, dark moons clamped
onto shell's sky, waiting for their tide.

NOTES ON THE POEMS

Running: German V-1 rockets were nicknamed "doodlebugs" (stanza 3, line 1).

Bach in the Garden: "To be free of all the hemmed-in life" (stanza 1, line 4) is taken from D. H. Lawrence's travel memoir *Sea and Sardinia* (1921).

Sonnet of Intimacy: This piece was suggested by Vinicius de Moraes's poem "Soneto de Intimidade" (1937).

Grief and Magritte: The word "yali" (stanza 8, line 1) refers to an old house or mansion on the banks of the Bosphorus.

    "Un objet fait supposer qu'il y en a d'autres derrière lui," which is quoted beginning in the penultimate line of the poem, translates to "an object makes us suppose there are others behind it." The phrase comes from Magritte's 1929 piece "Les mots et les images," which appeared in the journal *La révolution surréaliste*.

Why: The Latin phrase "spem in alium," which appears in line 3, is taken from the opening of the eponymous 1570 motet by composer Thomas Tallis. It translates to "hope in any other."

    The last line of the poem, "What remains when disbelief has gone," is quoted from Philip Larkin's "Church Going" (1954).

A Sleeping Rock: See Jonathan Edwards's essay "Of Being" (1721), particularly the passage that reads "when we go to expel body out of our thoughts, we must be sure not to leave empty space in the room of it . . . but we must think of the same that the sleeping rocks dream of, and not till then shall we get a complete idea of nothing."

ACKNOWLEDGMENTS

With thanks and gratitude to Grace Schulman and Wyatt Prunty. Thank
you also to Catherine Goldstead, Hilary Jacqmin, Magdalene Klassen, and
Kristina Lykke at Johns Hopkins University Press.

Some of the poems in this collection have appeared, sometimes with differ-
ent titles and in different versions, in the following publications:

Antioch Review: "North"

Caliban: "Pastoral"

Chicago Review: "Turtle Moon"

Commonweal: "Churchyard, "Bats"

Cumberland River Review: "The Same in All Directions"

Georgia Review: "History"

Gettysburg Review: "William Blake and Space Travel," "Bach in the Garden,"
    "Shopping for Snacks," "Sonnet of Intimacy"

Harvard Review: "Silence"

Hudson Review: "Composed"

Missouri Review: "The Silence," "Making Sense," "Serenade"

Plume: "The Garden"

Poet Lore: "Running"

Raritan: "The Passion"

Salmagundi: "Elegiac"

Stand: "The Dog"

World Literature Today: "Nationalism"

"Composed" was the recipient of a 2021 Pushcart Prize.

ABOUT THE AUTHOR

Brian Swann was born in Wallsend, England. He received his BA and MA from Queens' College, University of Cambridge, and his PhD from Princeton University, where he also taught. He has authored a novel, *Husakanaw*; several collections of short fiction and poetry (including *In Late Light*, published by Johns Hopkins University Press); and a number of volumes of poetry in translation and children's books. He is also the editor of several volumes of or on Native American literature, including *Wearing the Morning Star: Native American Song-Poems* and *Coming to Light: Contemporary Translations of the Native Literatures of North America*. The recipient of many writing awards, prizes, and fellowships, he lives in Manhattan, where he teaches at the Cooper Union.

POETRY TITLES IN THE SERIES

John Hollander, *Blue Wine and Other Poems*

Robert Pack, *Waking to My Name: New and Selected Poems*

Philip Dacey, *The Boy under the Bed*

Wyatt Prunty, *The Times Between*

Barry Spacks, *Spacks Street, New and Selected Poems*

Gibbons Ruark, *Keeping Company*

David St. John, *Hush*

Wyatt Prunty, *What Women Know, What Men Believe*

Adrien Stoutenberg, *Land of Superior Mirages: New and Selected Poems*

John Hollander, *In Time and Place*

Charles Martin, *Steal the Bacon*

John Bricuth, *The Heisenberg Variations*

Tom Disch, *Yes, Let's: New and Selected Poems*

Wyatt Prunty, *Balance as Belief*

Tom Disch, *Dark Verses and Light*

Thomas Carper, *Fiddle Lane*

Emily Grosholz, *Eden*

X. J. Kennedy, *Dark Horses: New Poems*

Wyatt Prunty, *The Run of the House*

Robert Phillips, *Breakdown Lane*

Vicki Hearne, *The Parts of Light*

Timothy Steele, *The Color Wheel*

Josephine Jacobsen, *In the Crevice of Time: New and Collected Poems*

Thomas Carper, *From Nature*

John Burt, *Work without Hope: Poetry by John Burt*

Charles Martin, *What the Darkness Proposes: Poems*

Wyatt Prunty, *Since the Noon Mail Stopped*

William Jay Smith, *The World below the Window: Poems 1937–1997*

Wyatt Prunty, *Unarmed and Dangerous: New and Selected Poems*

Robert Phillips, *Spinach Days*

X. J. Kennedy, *The Lords of Misrule: Poems 1992–2001*

John T. Irwin, ed., *Words Brushed by Music: Twenty-Five Years of the
    Johns Hopkins Poetry Series*

John Bricuth, *As Long As It's Big: A Narrative Poem*

Robert Phillips, *Circumstances Beyond Our Control: Poems*

Daniel Anderson, *Drunk in Sunlight*

X. J. Kennedy, *In a Prominent Bar in Secaucus: New and Selected Poems, 1955–2007*

William Jay Smith, *Words by the Water*

Wyatt Prunty, *The Lover's Guide to Trapping*

Charles Martin, *Signs & Wonders*

Peter Filkins, *The View We're Granted*

Brian Swann, *In Late Light*

Daniel Anderson, *The Night Guard at the Wilberforce Hotel*

Wyatt Prunty, *Couldn't Prove, Had to Promise*

John Bricuth, *Pure Products of America, Inc.*

X. J. Kennedy, *That Swing: Poems 2008–2016*

Charles Martin, *Future Perfect*

Hastings Hensel, *Ballyhoo*

Sidney Wade, *Deep Gossip: New and Selected Poems*

Peter Filkins, *Water / Music*

Brian Swann, *Imago*